I0435317

Contents

Introduction   1

U. S. Arctic Region Policy   3

Single GCC for the Arctic Region   6

      Effective Interaction with Arctic Council   9

      Ensuring Command Overlay   12

      USEUCOM as Arctic GCC   14

Conclusion and Recommendations   16

Illustrations   18

Bibliography   19

Abstract

The United States is now taking the necessary steps toward protecting its national economic and strategic interests within the Arctic region. The first step was the release of the Arctic Regional Policy (ARP) by President Bush prior to leaving office in January of 2009. This set clear priorities regarding the region, which the United States must now determine how to achieve. This paper addresses the next two steps in the process to secure these objectives. The first will be the need to ratify the United Nations Convention on the Law of the Sea (UNCLOS) and thereby have legal validity to our territorial claims within the Arctic. The second step will be to identify which Geographic Combatant Commander (GCC) should have responsibility over the region. Currently there are three GCCs that have portions of the regions within their areas of responsibility (AORs). This current structure creates confusion among the GCCs and leaves seams available to be exploited by other nations. By assigning USEUCOM the entire Arctic Region and then establishing an Arctic Sub-Unified Commander under it, the United States will assume the leadership role that other nations have come to expect. The United States understands that it must leverage all aspects of military and political influence ensure the priorities of National Security Presidential Directive 66 identifies, and USEUCOM is the most capable GCC of achieving that objective.

INTRODUCTION

International awareness regarding the Arctic Circle continues to grow due to increasing polar ice melt, and the need to identify how that region will be handled by the United States is becoming more evident. The region has been transformed into a maelstrom of competing commercial, national security and environmental concerns with profound implications for the international legal and political system."[1] The ice melt has created opportunities for Arctic countries to expand their territorial areas for access to more natural resources. Those resources range from mineral and deposit exploration to fishing. Each of these has the potential to greatly affect their economies. The warmer waters are bringing fish up further north than ever seen before" states then Navy Commander Ray Chartier, National Ice Center Director, in his *Sea Power* interview of October 2007.[2]

The need to establish a national policy and a seamless command structure regarding the Arctic Region could not be more important.[3] Of the eight members of the Arctic Council, seven are not only signatories but have also ratified the United Nations Conventional Law of the Sea (UNCLOS), while the United States is the lone member who has not ratified the treaty.[4] These nations are continuing to stake claims regarding their territorial waters through UNCLOS while the United States is unable to make a valid claim because it is not a party to the treaty. As each of these countries begins to vie for control over portions of that region, tensions could begin to rise. The need to establish a lasting peace

---

[1] Charles K. Ebinger and Evie Zambetakis. The geopolitics of Arctic melt." *International Affairs.* London. Vol. 85, Iss. 6, (November 2009): 1215-1232.

[2] Richard R. Burgess. The New Cold War?" *Sea Power*, October 2007.

[3] For the purposes of this paper, the Arctic Region will be defined as the area north of 70°N Latitude Line.

[4] United Nations Conventional Law of the Sea (UNCLOS) Signatory Status http://www.un.org/Depts/los/LEGISLATIONANDTREATIES/status htm. (accessed March 8, 2010).

and stability in the region is now more important than ever, before they escalate any higher. The United States cannot afford to ignore this region any longer.

Currently the Arctic Region falls under three separate Geographic Combatant Commanders (GCCs): U.S. European Command (USEUCOM), U.S. Pacific Command (USPACOM), and U.S. Northern Command (USNORTHCOM) (See Figure 1).[5] Some of the questions that must be addressed are: Will it remain as it is under the current Unified Command Plan (UCP)? Will DOD restructure and create another Geographic Combatant Commander? Or will the Arctic fall under a current GCC and establish an Arctic Sub-Unified Commander? One possible solution is to form an entirely new GCC to focus on the Arctic, but this may be construed in a negative light by the other Arctic Nations.[6] The DOD should be mindful of giving the impression that the United States is making illegitimate territorial claims within the Arctic Circle by creating the impression that the United States sees military might rather than diplomacy as the best approach to protecting its Arctic interests. The best option would be to create a single Arctic Commander under an already established GCC. By assigning USEUCOM the entire Arctic Region and then establishing an Arctic Sub-Unified Commander under it, the United States will assume the leadership role that other nations have come to expect. As the Arctic Circle becomes a region with greater global importance than in the past, it is imperative to determine how the United States will oversee and monitor that region. Though there are multiple options, USEUCOM is the one that is most logical due to its relative influence with the other countries that also have national interests invested within that area.

---

[5] U.S. President. *Unified Command Plan*. Washington D.C: The White House, 17 December 2008. (FOUO)
[6] William P. Hayes, CAPT, SC, USN. ―The Arctic: One Region, One Commander", Naval War College, Newport, RI, 23 October 2003.

The region is inextricably interconnected and the decision of one nation affects the others in economic, political, and social ways. This is the challenge that the United States faces, as it tries to protect its own claims while respecting and honoring those of its neighboring countries. NSPD-66 identifies the Department of State (DOS) as the lead agency but will look to many of its sister agencies as well as the other Arctic Nations to assist in accomplishing this charter. The Department of Defense (DOD) will be one of those departments that will be relied upon heavily.[7] In order for the DOD to best address this situation, it must determine the various courses of action available and then narrow them down to the one that helps to best accomplish the goal. Implicit in this discussion of alternatives is deciding who will have responsibility for the Arctic Region.

As General Victor Renuart, Commander U.S. Northern Command (USNORTHCOM), stated: ―any time nations converge on an area to either compete for or collectively mine natural resources, there is a possibility…that their interests will not coincide.‖[8] It is time for the United States to start looking for how to best address this situation.

U. S. ARCTIC REGION POLICY

On January 9, 2009, then President George W. Bush signed into effect National Security Presidential Directive 66 (NSPD-66) and Homeland Security Presidential Directive 25 (HSPD-25). President George W. Bush clearly identified the direction our nation needs to take regarding the Arctic region and the actions needed in order to implement this new

---

[7] George W. Bush, ―National Security Presidential Directive and Homeland Security Presidential Directive: NSPD-66 / HSPD-25.‖ The White House. January 9, 2009.
[8] ―U.S. Military Wants Fresh Look At Arctic Policy.‖ *Defense Daily*. Potomac. December 18, 2008. Vol. 240, Iss. 53.

policy.[9] Over fifteen years have passed since the previous Arctic Region Policy (ARP) was issued and a great deal has changed over the course of time. The ARP is specific regarding the responsibilities of each of the agencies charged with carrying out the policy. Those agencies include the Departments of Defense, State, Homeland Security, Commerce, Energy, and the Interior.[10] This broad spectrum of responsibility serves to illustrate the notion that this region is an area of rapidly growing concern. The new ARP is only the first step that must be taken in order to secure U.S. national interests within the region.

As the United States tries to catch up with the rest of the Arctic countries, they continue to press for reform through the United Nations (UN) and the Law of the Sea convention. The sooner this issue is resolved, the sooner those countries who have submitted claims can begin to act. Each nation has a vested interest in a speedy solution. Canada is seeking to protect its economic prosperity via the Northwest Passage, the Russian Federation is looking to expand its already dominant real estate within the Arctic Circle, and Norway wants to protect its claims surrounding the Norwegian Sea, while Denmark is looking to expand its nation's natural resources.[11] Though Sweden and Finland are landlocked to the north and unable to make territorial water claims within in the region, they still have a vested interest in the results of each of the other countries' claims. Iceland, who is also interested in those results, is not claiming any territory within the disputed region and, therefore, poses no concern to any of the Arctic nations.[12]

---

[9] George W. Bush, ―National Security Presidential Directive and Homeland Security Presidential Directive: NSPD-66 / HSPD-25." The White House. January 9, 2009.
[10] George W. Bush, ―National Security Presidential Directive and Homeland Security Presidential Directive: NSPD-66 / HSPD-25." The White House. January 9, 2009.
[11] Thomas Omestad. ―The Race for the Arctic, As the ice melts, nations eye oil and gas deposits and shipping routes," *U.S. News and World Report*, Vol. 145, Iss. 8, pg. 53.
[12] Norwegian Ministry of Foreign Affairs.
―Norway's Policy in the High North – the Arctic Dimension". http://www regjeringen no/en/dep/ud/

The policy encompasses a broad spectrum of interests to include: national and homeland security interests in the Arctic; international governance; extended continental shelf and boundary issues; maritime transportation in the arctic region; economic issues, including energy; and environmental protection and conservation of natural resources.[13] Each of these themes are evidence of the overarching importance of the region and how U.S. national interests need to be protected through the implementation of a policy that addresses such a broad scope of concerns.

As the lead, DOS will look to leverage international organizations and bilateral contracts to promote U.S. interests in the Arctic.[14] Additionally, it will call upon the skill sets of many of other departments and agencies to ensure stability and U.S. credibility within the region. One of the major U.S. agencies to play a role in the implementation of this policy, aside from the DOD, is the Department of Homeland Security (DHS). The ARP requires that the DOS and DHS work in conjunction and coordination with heads of other relevant executive departments and agencies in order to:

- Develop greater capabilities and capacity to protect U.S. air, land, and sea borders within the Arctic region
- Increase Arctic maritime domain awareness to protect maritime commerce, critical infrastructure, and key resources
- Preserve global mobility of U.S. vessels and aircraft throughout the region
- Project a sovereign U.S. maritime presence in support of essential U.S. interests
- Encourage peaceful resolution of disputes within the region[15]

These five priorities are intended to focus the efforts of all departments and agencies in protecting the interests of the United States.

---

[13] George W. Bush, ⌐National Security Presidential Directive and Homeland Security Presidential Directive: NSPD-66 / HSPD-25." The White House. January 9, 2009.
[14] Ibid.
[15] Ibid.

Though there are multiple agencies that will play prominent roles in accomplishing these priorities, no single agency will play a dominant one. With that being said, the DOD's responsibility during this transition has the potential to be extremely influential since it possesses capabilities that no other agency can provide to execute this policy. Establishing a single source of authority regarding this region would be the most effective method of implementation. A single GCC in charge of the Arctic would be able to identify the basing and logistical requirements as well as assist U.S. Government (USG) agencies in addressing each of the others concerns.

SINGLE GCC FOR THE ARCTIC REGION

The 2008 Unified Command Plan divides the world among seven GCCs with responsibility for the Arctic Region shared among three separate GCCs, unlike the Antarctic which is controlled by only one.[16] USNORTHCOM, USPACOM, and USEUCOM all have a certain level of responsibility which translates into the potential to be identified as the lead GCC. USEUCOM's mission statement identifies its role by the following, ―U.S. European Command conducts military operations, international military partnering, and interagency partnering to enhance transatlantic security and defend the United States forward."[17] According to USNORTHCOM's mission statement, ―USNORTHCOM anticipates and conducts Homeland Defense and Civil Support operations within the assigned area of responsibility to defend, protect, and secure the United States and its interests."[18] Likewise, ―USPACOM protects and defends, in concert with other U.S. Government agencies, the

[16] Unified Command Plan homepage. http://www.defense.gov/specials/unifiedcommand/
[17] USEUCOM homepage. http://www.eucom.mil/
[18] USNORTHCOM homepage. http://www.northcom.mil/

territory of the United States, its people, and its interests."[19] Each of these commanders

views the Arctic as an area of interest within their realm of responsibility. The Command

and Control (C2) aspects that encompass such a vast region will be difficult challenges to

address as the relative interest in the region continues to grow.

Though each of these commanders have identified U.S. national interests as vital

aspects of their mission, the amount of coordination required to address any concerns within

the region will only lead to a lack of timeliness. This unnecessary division could cause

confusion when circumstances require an immediate solution be implemented towards a

volatile situation. In order to address this seam in C2, the United States should identify a

single current GCC to have sole purview over that region. It should also establish a new sub-

unified commander, under that same GCC, to give the Arctic the focus and attention it

requires. An example of this concept can be found within the UCP regarding Antarctica.

USPACOM is the sole GCC to have Antarctica and the South Pole within its AOR. This

same concept could be applied to the Arctic Region. By looking at the UCP and the

associated lines of longitude assigned to each GCC, it can be determined that currently

USNORTHCOM is responsible for a little over 25% of the region, USPACOM is responsible

for a little over 34%, and USEUCOM oversees greater than 40% of the Arctic Region.[20]

USNORTHCOM currently works closely with North American Aerospace Defense

Command (NORAD) and addresses all Homeland Defense operations. Many may argue that

because of this relationship, USNORTHCOM should take the lead on this. However,

Homeland Defense is not the sole issue at stake in the Arctic. The ARP stresses the

---

[19] USPACOM homepage. http://www.pacom.mil/
[20] Unified Command Plan homepage. http://www.defense.gov/specials/unifiedcommand/

importance of protecting maritime commerce and with the opening of both the Northeast and

Northwest trade passages, the potential for more efficient trade routes exist.[21] There is also

the concern regarding the unresolved boundary that the United States has with Canada in the

Beaufort Sea.[22] As Canada falls under USNORTHCOM's area of responsibility, it could

create unnecessary tension if USNORTHCOM were given complete control over the region

and should be avoided as best as possible. As General Renuart, Commander

USNORTHCOM commented, ―the two neighbors don't always see eye-to-eye on how

territorial waters are delineated.‖[23]

Within its area of responsibility regarding this region, USPACOM only has non-

Arctic nations that are deeply interested in energy resources or shorter shipping distances and

therefore should not be the lead either. USPACOM is the sole GCC for the Antarctic, and by

assigning the Arctic region to a USEUCOM under a single Arctic sub-unified command it

would allow the United States to have a commander responsible for each of the two poles.[24]

Countries such as Japan and China have both invested in icebreakers, but due to their

geographical location are unable to stake territorial claims within the region.[25] China has

even established a research center within the region.[26] Their interest and involvement are

cause for concern and should be monitored as things progress. Though both China and Japan

---

[21] Icelandic Government. ―Breaking the Ice‖ Conference Report. Akureyri, March 27-28, 2007.
www.mfa.is/media/.../Breaking_The_Ice_Conference_Report.pdf
[22] George W. Bush, ―National Security Presidential Directive and Homeland Security Presidential Directive:
NSPD-66 / HSPD-25.‖ The White House. January 9, 2009.
[23] ―U.S. Military Wants Fresh Look At Arctic Policy.‖ *Defense Daily*. Potomac. December 18, 2008.
Vol. 240, Iss. 53
[24] Unified Command Plan homepage. http://www.defense.gov/specials/unifiedcommand/
[25] Mark Galeotti. ―Cold Calling-Competition heats us for Arctic resources‖, *Jane's, Jane's Intelligence Review*.
September 18, 2008.
[26] Ibid.

have understandable interests, such interests are not so noteworthy as to justify identifying USPACOM as the Arctic GCC.

USEUCOM has 75% of the Arctic Council nations within its AOR, as well as three of the five Arctic Nations. Therefore, it would be able to capitalize upon those bonds that have been forged over time to help ensure peace and stability within the region. USEUCOM should take advantage of the ability to be able to work within existing institutions.[27] The Northeast Passage will open the world to never before seen speed and efficiency regarding the delivery of goods from one side of the world to the other. This passage will traverse the region along Russia's northern border toward the Norwegian Sea and reduce the distance by over 40%.[28] Because of the geographical responsibility that is already entrusted to USEUCOM, as well as its personal relationships with six of the other seven Arctic Council nations, it is the most logical choice to be chosen as the lead for this much needed region.

Effective Interaction with Arctic Council

If the United States leaves those Arctic Region seams unaddressed, it could be perceived by the international community as indifference. The United States must present not only a united front but a confident one. This will reassure the other members of the Arctic Council of its dedication to ensuring stability and to strengthen institutions for cooperation among the eight Arctic nations."[29] The United States needs to assure those countries that it is truly dedicated to stability within the region. One of the most effective

---

[27] Charles K. Ebinger and Evie Zambetakis. "The geopolitics of Arctic melt." *International Affairs.* London. Vol. 85, Iss. 6, (November 2009): 1215-1232.
[28] Norwegian Ministry of Foreign Affairs. "Norway's Policy in the High North – the Arctic Dimension". http://www.regjeringen.no/en/dep/ud/
[29] George W. Bush, "National Security Presidential Directive and Homeland Security Presidential Directive: NSPD-66 / HSPD-25." The White House. January 9, 2009.

ways to accomplish this is to fill those seams and identify a single military director to give it the attention it deserves. The United States currently has very strong ties and relationships with the Arctic countries and needs to continue to improve upon them.

One of Admiral James Stavridis', Commander USEUCOM, top priorities is to build upon the military-to-military relationship the United States already has established with Russia.[30] In a recent interview, he stresses the importance of maintaining and building upon those relationships that exist between the United States and members of the Arctic Council. The United States must be cognizant of Russia's motives, as it seeks to build upon its realm of influence within the region. In order to best accomplish this objective, the United States should seek to leverage USEUCOM's personal, political, and military connections regarding that country and as well as any other in the region.

United States and Norwegian ties are stronger than ever as they continue to improve upon decades of cooperation and respect. This relationship is one of many that USEUCOM must capitalize on to help maintain peace within the region while securing U.S. national interests. Norway seeks to solidify its claims extending into the Norwegian Sea off the mainland coast as well as Svalbard, a Norwegian island located within the Arctic Circle and the Barents Sea.[31] Concurrently it is concerned with the area of overlapping claims between Norway and the Russian Federation.[32] Norway is dedicated to ensuring all territorial claims are resolved in a peaceful and legal manner.

---

[30] ADM James Stavridis interview with AFN on April 14, 2010.
http://www.youtube.com/watch?v=S9BMBqRk0ac&feature=autoshare
[31] Arctic Map see http://www.athropolis.com/map2.htm
[32] Norwegian Ministry of Petroleum and Energy http://www.regjeringen.no/en/dep/oed.html?id=750

Sweden and Finland are unable to stake claims to any extension of their territorial waters into the Arctic region due to being landlocked between Norway and the Russian Federation. They do however still have a vested interest regarding regional stability. Iceland is currently not making any claims within the Arctic Region and therefore is not directly involved in any territorial disputes.[33] Along with all the other Arctic Council nations, it will look toward the United States for reassurance and support regarding regional stability. This support is necessary due to the strong voice the United States has within NATO. NATO is concerned with the entire region as well as the ―possibility of deteriorating relations between Russia and the West."[34]

Another example of the importance of this region, as well as the visibility it is receiving on the international stage, is through the upcoming meeting of the Arctic nations.[35] The five Arctic nations will meet this coming May [2010], in Greenland to discuss territorial claims in the Arctic, as well as the topics of accidents and oil spills and the effects that changes in the region will have on the indigenous people living there. Along with those topics, the Arctic seabed will be the most widely discussed topic as the warming climate makes it more accessible for exploration of oil and mineral resources.[36]

---

[33] Norwegian Ministry of Foreign Affairs. ―Norway's Policy in the High North – the Arctic Dimension". http://www.regjeringen.no/en/dep/ud/
[34] ―NATO Parliamentary Assembly Discusses Alliance Role in High North." *Defense Daily International*, May 29, 2009.
[35] The five Arctic nations include; the United States, Canada, the Russian Federation, Norway, and Denmark (Greenland).
[36] Polar Conservation Organization. http://www.polarconservation.org

Ensuring Command Overlay

Joint Publication 3-0 (JP 3-0) states that ―combatant commanders are instrumental in unifying the actions between military and non-military units to achieve unity of effort.‖[37] In order to achieve the required unity of effort within this region, the United States is taking the necessary steps to address this concern. The most effective way is to ensure a clear command structure exists and to eliminate the geographical seams. These seams are located along the longitudinal lines of 45°W, 100°E, and 169°W. The mere existence of these seams could promote confusion and concern regarding which GCC would be responsible for addressing a national interest issue that spans more than one AOR. Because of these potential situations, those seams should be eliminated immediately in order to put forth a united front and a single face to the region.

Not only do the geographical seams need to be removed but the political ones as well. The eight Arctic Council nations are divided between two of the three GCCs responsible for the Arctic Region. USNORTHCOM's area of responsibility encompasses the United States and Canada. Canada is the only Arctic nation within USNORTHCOM's AOR that has both signed and ratified UNCLOS and therefore whose territorial claims will be recognized by the international community. The United States is still looking to ratify the law in the Senate.[38] Canada, along with the United States, is a member of a number of political councils. They include: the Arctic Council, NATO, and the UN.[39] (See Table I). These relationships illustrate the amount of influence Canada has throughout the international community

---

[37] Chairman, U.S. Joint Chiefs of Staff. *Joint Operations.* ―JP 3-0‖. Washington DC: CJCS, 2008. Pg. xiii.

[38] ―U.S. Military Wants Fresh Look At Arctic Policy.‖ *Defense Daily.* Potomac. December 18, 2008. Vol. 240, Iss. 53

[39] For a list of NATO member countries see http://www.nato.int/cps/en/natolive/nato_countries.htm. For a list of members of the United Nations see http://www.un.org/

through various avenues such as the Northwest Passage and other sea lanes that traverse the Arctic Circle within Canada's territorial waters.

USEUCOM, however, is responsible for the remaining six countries that are members of the Arctic Council: Denmark, Finland, Iceland, Norway, the Russian Federation, and Sweden. Each of these countries, much like Canada and the United States, are members of multiple councils ranging from NATO, the European Union (EU), to the UN. In addition to having a voice within multiple multinational councils, these members are UNCLOS signatories as well.[40] Denmark, Finland and Sweden are EU members, while the members of NATO include Demark, Iceland, and Norway. [41] (See Table I).

Arctic Region Nations	Arctic Council	NATO	EU	UN	UNCLOS Signatory	EUCOM	NORTHCOM
United States	X	X		X			X
Canada	X	X		X	11-Jul-03		X
Denmark	X	X	X	X	16-Nov-04	X	
Finland	X		X	X	21-Jun-96	X	
Iceland	X	X		X	21-Jun-85	X	
Norway	X	X		X	24-Jun-96	X	
Russian Federation	X			X	3-Dec-97	X	
Sweden	X		X	X	25-Jun-96	X	

Table I. Council Membership Chart

Each of these councils and the memberships to them, require the United States to have a great deal of understanding of the underlying political message each membership sends to the international community. It is within U.S. national interests to invest the necessary effort

---

[40] United Nations homepage. http://www.un.org/
[41] For a list of European Union Countries see http://www.eucountrylist.com. For a list of NATO member countries see http://www nato.int/cps/en/natolive/nato_countries htm

toward cultivating stronger relationships across all the boundaries of those political seams. Since USEUCOM is responsible for those six countries and has established lasting relationships with them for over 50 years, it has been able to promote the necessary effort to ―integrate interagency, academia, NGOs, IOs, and private sector partners to better execute the EUCOM mission through a ‗Whole of Government Approach'" through European Command's Interagency Partnering Staff (ECJ9).[42]

USEUCOM as Arctic GCC

Once the entire Arctic is within its AOR, USEUCOM will be able to maneuver effectively in order to best meet the needs of the United States and its neighboring Arctic nations. As the polar ice cap continues to melt, it will open up more accessible waterways to northern Russia, through use of the Northeast Passage, as well as along Canada and the Northwest Passage. These routes will significantly change trade routes in the future as ―the Northern Sea Route cuts the distance between Russian Atlantic and Pacific ports by 40%."[43] With the increased influence the Russian Federation will have with the opening of the Northeast Passage, it is imperative that the United States establish an Arctic Command to effectively address the impact this will have on the region while maintaining the United States ability to project sea power throughout the region.[44] While trying to address the growing interest that Russia is placing upon the Arctic, the United States must also be aware of the ripple effect Russia's interest will have throughout the Arctic nations. Russia's

[42] USEUCOM homepage. http://www.eucom mil/
[43] Icelandic Government. ―Breaking the Ice" Conference Report. Akureyri, March 27-28, 2007. www.mfa.is/media/.../Breaking_The_Ice_Conference_Report.pdf
[44] George W. Bush. ―National Security Presidential Directive and Homeland Security Presidential Directive: NSPD-66 / HSPD-25." The White House. January 9, 2009.

interest in the Northeast Passage is one of intrigue that must be monitored very closely.[45] The United States must be prepared for the political and economic impact of this inevitability. USEUCOM is the best choice for leading that charter.

In order to support U.S. strategic and economic objectives, USEUCOM would need to coordinate with all the nations within the region to address their joint interests. Currently the world's nations have their eyes on a very different area of concern in U.S. Central Command (USCENTCOM), but if the United States continues to ignore the importance of the Arctic Region it will be "reacting" to the situation instead of being a driving force. If the United States is able to establish a viable presence within the region, it will be able to build upon the level of knowledge it currently has regarding the environment, regional security, the indigenous people and the effect globalization will have on their livelihood, as well as all of its national interests concerning that region.

USEUCOM should be tasked to stand up the new Arctic Subunified Command. It will also need to take into account the tools necessary to improve upon its military might within that arena as well as how to ensure it creates a sense of transparency towards the other Arctic nations. By establishing this transparency and openness and the ability to strengthen the bonds of trust the United States has with the Arctic nations will help in achieving stability and success.

One of those military requirements, that will need to be addressed, is the ice-breaker fleet the U.S. Coast Guard (USCG) currently has in its inventory. At this time the USCG only has three ice-breakers of which only two are able to handle the thickness of the Arctic

---

[45] "NATO Parliamentary Assembly Discusses Alliance Role in High North." *Defense Daily International*, May 29, 2009.

ice.[46] If left unaddressed, the United States will be unable to explore deep into its territorial claims which will limit its domain awareness. This critical vulnerability is one that will need to quickly be addressed before USEUCOM would assume full responsibility of the region. The United States must be able to exercise its influence in the Arctic if it intends to be able to voice and protect its national economic and strategic interests. USEUCOM will need to establish and maintain the necessary political and military relationships in order to minimize and de-escalate any ―existing and potential conflicts of interest in the area which could undermine the High North‘s stability.‖[47]

CONCLUSION and RECOMMENDATIONS

As the Arctic begins to experience the changes of ice melt and the surrounding nations reap the benefits as a result, it will also undergo vast changes in its ecological sustainment. This concern is only one of many identified in the NSPD-66.[48]

The most effective way of addressing these concerns is for the United States to establish an Arctic Sub-Unified Commander, preferably under an already recognized GCC. The logical GCC would be USEUCOM as it already has strong significant ties to all but one of the Arctic Nations, Canada.

While the United States is establishing this new subordinate commander, it must also quickly resolve the issues that surround UNCLOS and ratify the law. This will allow for the United States to submit territorial claims that would extend to the end of the continental shelf

---

[46] Patricia Kime. ―Men: U.S. policy on Arctic needs update.‖ *Navy Times*. Springfield.
October 8, 2007: 28.
[47] ―NATO Parliamentary Assembly Discusses Alliance Role in High North.‖
Defense Daily International, May 29, 2009. The Arctic Region is also known by many European countries as the High North.
[48] George W. Bush. ―National Security Presidential Directive and Homeland Security
Presidential Directive: NSPD-66 / HSPD-25.‖ The White House. January 9, 2009.

off of Alaska. If the United States continues to choose to not ratify the law, then it would be unable submit a claim to the commission and enjoy the international recognition and certainty that parties to the convention enjoy.[49] This process will directly influence the economic stability and research/resource exploration initiatives that the United States deems necessary toward securing its interests.[50]

The United States needs to protect these interests within the region, and the most effective way to accomplish this is to create an organization directly responsible for meeting the five priorities that the ARP laid out. By creating an Arctic Sub-Unified Command that is able to traverse the interagency bridges necessary to achieve these goals, the United States will not only secure its national interests within the region but also display a clear sense of support and genuine concern for the many mutual interests the Arctic nations share. Though USNORTHCOM is responsible for homeland defense and works closely with DHS, it would not the best choice due to its lack of intimate knowledge of six of the Arctic nations. USPACOM only has other non-Arctic nations who are only deeply interested in energy resources and shorter shipping distances. These are not strong enough reasons to select USPACOM as the lead either. USEUCOM has direct relationships with each of these countries and understands the concerns that they have raised. It is imperative that the United States shore up these seams in C2 as well as its political interests and take a more holistic approach to the region. The most effective way of accomplishing this is by the establishment of an Arctic sub-unified command under USEUCOM. By building upon these relationships, USEUCOM can gain a better understanding of each of the Arctic nations' desires and how it can aid them in achieving their goals while still protecting its own security and interests.

---

[49] Burgess, Richard R. ―The New Cold War?‖ *Sea Power*, October 2007.
[50] George W. Bush. ―National Security Presidential Directive and Homeland Security Presidential Directive: NSPD-66 / HSPD-25.‖ The White House. January 9, 2009.

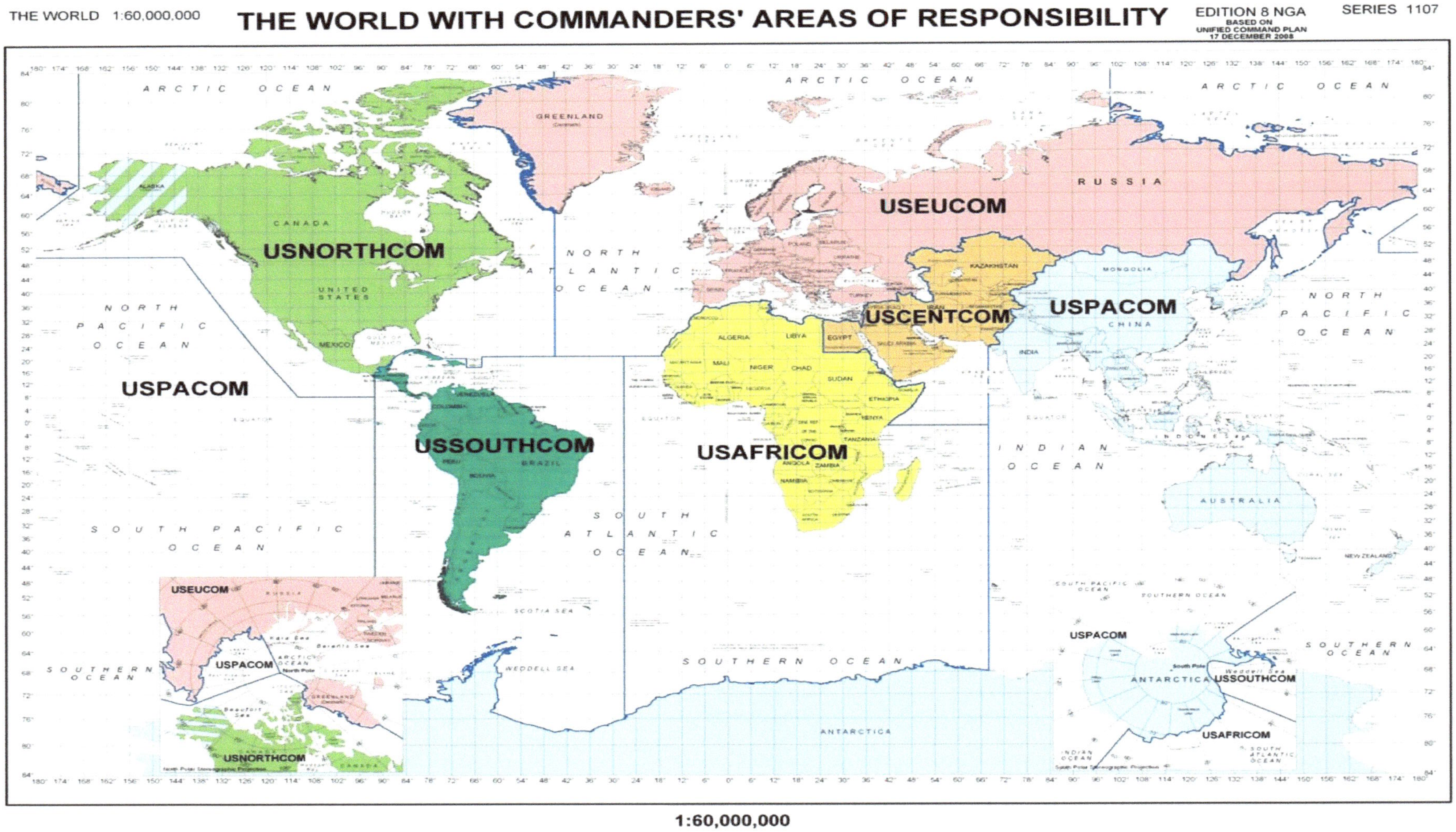
THE WORLD 1:60,000,000
THE WORLD WITH COMMANDERS' AREAS OF RESPONSIBILITY
EDITION 8 NGA
BASED ON
UNIFIED COMMAND PLAN
17 DECEMBER 2008
SERIES 1107
ARCTIC OCEAN
GREENLAND
RUSSIA
USEUCOM
USNORTHCOM
CANADA
UNITED STATES
MEXICO
NORTH ATLANTIC OCEAN
NORTH PACIFIC OCEAN
USPACOM
USCENTCOM
KAZAKHSTAN
MONGOLIA
CHINA
INDIA
EGYPT
ALGERIA
LIBYA
MALI
NIGER
CHAD
SUDAN
ETHIOPIA
KENYA
TANZANIA
ANGOLA
ZAMBIA
NAMIBIA
USAFRICOM
USSOUTHCOM
BRAZIL
INDIAN OCEAN
AUSTRALIA
NEW ZEALAND
SOUTH PACIFIC OCEAN
SOUTH ATLANTIC OCEAN
SCOTIA SEA
WEDDELL SEA
SOUTHERN OCEAN
ANTARCTICA
North Pole
South Pole
1:60,000,000

FIGURE 1

BIBLIOGRAPHY

Arctic Council. http://www.arctic-council.org/ (accessed February 24, 2010).

Arctic Map. http://www.athropolis.com/map2.htm (accessed April 16, 2010).

Assorted illustrations for the Arctic Council (Figures IV and V).
	http://maps.grida.no/go/collection/assorted-illustrations-for-the-arctic-council
	(accessed February 24, 2010).

Blunden, Margaret. ―The New Problem of Arctic Stability." *Survival.* Vol. 51, Iss. 5,
	(October 1, 2009): 121. http://www.proquest.com/ (accessed February 22, 2010).

Brigham, Lawson W. ―Thinking about the Arctic's Future: Scenarios for 2040." *The
	Futurist.* Washington. Vol. 41, Iss. 5, (September 2007.): 27-29, 31-34.
	http://www.proquest.com/ (accessed February 22, 2010).

Burgess, Richard R. ―The New Cold War?" *Sea Power*, October 2007.
	http://www.proquest.com/ (accessed February 22, 2010).

Bush, George W. ―National Security Presidential Directive and Homeland Security
	Presidential Directive: NSPD-66 / HSPD-25." *The White House.* January 9, 2009.
	http://www.fas.org/irp/offdocs/nspd/nspd-66.htm (accessed February 22, 2010).

Commander's Areas of Responsibility Illustration (Figure I).
	http://www.defense.gov/home/features/2009/0109_unifiedcommand/
	(accessed February 22, 2010).

Crook, John R. ―Comprehensive New Statement of U.S. Arctic Policy." *The American
	Journal Of International Law*. Vol. 103, Iss. 2, (April 2009.): 342-349.
	http://www.proquest.com/ (accessed February 22, 2010).

Ebinger, Charles K. and Evie Zambetakis. ―The geopolitics of Arctic melt." *International
	Affairs.* London. Vol. 85, Iss. 6, (November 2009): 1215-1232.
	http://www.proquest.com/ (accessed February 22, 2010).

EUROPA – The Official website of the European Union. http://www.europa.eu/
	(accessed February 24, 2010).

Galeotti, Mark. ―Cold Calling-Competition heats us for Arctic resources", *Jane's, Jane's
	Intelligence Review.* September 18, 2008. http://www.janes.com
	(accessed March 18, 2010).

Golosov, R.. 2006. Opening Up the Arctic Region and Russia's Submarine Fleet. *Military*

Thought. Vol. 15, Iss. 2, (April 1): 177-184. http://www.proquest.com/ (accessed February 22, 2010).

Hayes , William P. CAPT, SC, USN. ―The Arctic: One Region, One Commander", Naval War College, Newport, RI. October 23, 2003.

Icelandic Government. ―Breaking the Ice" Conference Report. Akureyri, March 27-28, 2007. www.mfa.is/media/.../Breaking_The_Ice_Conference_Report.pdf. (accessed April 22, 2010).

International Maritime Organization homepage. http://www.imo.org/ (accessed March 5, 2010).

Kime, Patricia. ―Allen: U.S. policy on Arctic needs update." *Navy Times.* Springfield. October 8, 2007: 28. http://www.proquest.com/ (accessed February 22, 2010).

Kolodkin,A. and S Glandin. ―The Russian Flag on the North Pole." *International Affairs.* Vol. 53, Iss. 6, (December 1, 2007): 6-16. http://www.proquest.com/ (accessed February 22, 2010).

List of European Union Countries (Figure III). http://www.eucountrylist.com/ (accessed February 24, 2010).

Murgatroyd, C. ―Defense And The Arctic - Go With The Floe?" *RUSI Journal*, August 1, 2009: 82. http://www.proquest.com/ (accessed February 22, 2010).

NATO member countries http://www.nato.int/cps/en/natolive/nato_countries.htm (accessed February 24, 2010).

NATO member countries (Figure II). http://www.mapsofworld.com/images/maps-of-world-nato-member-countries.gif (accessed February 24, 2010).

―NATO Parliamentary Assembly Discusses Alliance Role in High North." *Defense Daily International*, May 29, 2009. http://www.proquest.com/ (accessed February 22, 2010).

―Northeast Passage". The Columbia Encyclopedia, Sixth Edition, 2008. http://www.encyclopedia.com/topic/Northeast_Passage.aspx (accessed April 16, 2010).

Norwegian Ministry of Petroleum and Energy. http://www.regjeringen.no/en/dep/oed.html?id=750 (accessed April 16, 2010).

Norwegian Ministry of Foreign Affairs.
    ―Norway's Policy in the High North – the Arctic Dimension".
    http://www.regjeringen.no/en/dep/ud/ (accessed April 16, 2010).

Omestad, Thomas. ―Bush Signs Off on New U.S. Arctic Policy." *US News and World*
    Report. January 12, 2009. http://www.proquest.com/ (accessed February 22, 2010).

―――. ―The Race for the Arctic, As the ice melts, nations eye oil and gas
    deposits and shipping routes," *U.S. News and World Report*, Vol. 145, Iss. 8, pg. 53.
    http://www.proquest.com/ (accessed March 18, 2010.)

Patterson, B. ―PRC Expedition Highlights Growing Importance of Polar Regions." *Defense*
    & Foreign Affairs Strategic Policy. November 1, 2007: 24.
    http://www.proquest.com/ (accessed February 22, 2010).

Polar Conservation Organization. http://www.polarconservation.org
    (accessed April 16, 2010).

―Rep. Larsen calls to Strengthen Coast Guard's Icebreaking Fleet to Protect Maritime Safety,
    American Interests in Arctic Region." *US Fed News Service, Including US State*
    News. July 16, 2008. http://www.proquest.com/ (accessed February 22, 2010).

Stavridis, James interview with AFN. (April 14, 2010).
    http://www.youtube.com/watch?v=S9BMBqRk0ac&feature=autoshare
    (accessed April 16, 2010).

UNCLOS Signatory Status
    http://www.un.org/Depts/los/LEGISLATIONANDTREATIES/status.htm
    (accessed March 8, 2010).

Unified Command Plan homepage. http://www.defense.gov/specials/unifiedcommand/
    (accessed February 22, 2010).

United Nations homepage. http://www.un.org/ (accessed March 3, 2010).

USEUCOM homepage. http://www.eucom.mil/ (accessed February 22, 2010).

USNORTHCOM homepage. http://www.northcom.mil/ (accessed February 22, 2010).

USPACOM homepage. http://www.pacom.mil/ (accessed February 22, 2010).

―U.S. Military Wants Fresh Look At Arctic Policy." *Defense Daily.* Potomac.
    December 18, 2008. Vol. 240, Iss. 53. http://www.proquest.com/
    (accessed February 22, 2010).

U.S. Office of the Chairman of the Joint Chiefs of Staff. *Joint Operations.* JP 3-0".
    Washington DC: CJCS, 2008. Pg. xiii.

U.S. President. *Unified Command Plan.* Washington D.C: The White House.
    December 17, 2008. (FOUO). (accessed April 9, 2010).

USEUCOM: Global and Theater Strategic End States (U), Guidance for Employment of the
    Force. 2008. Pg. 143. (Secret) Information extracted is unclassified.
    (accessed April 12, 2010).

www.ingramcontent.com/pod-product-compliance
Lightning Source LLC
Chambersburg PA
CBHW060821290526
45792CB00005BB/1750